JUST HAVE FAITH- MEMORIES FROM THE REAL WORLD

KAAVYAA GUPTA

To my everything: Reynah Gupta, Kavita Jain, Deepak Gupta and S.K. Gupta

Because they are the kind of people poems should be composed for, songs should be written about, and books should be dedicated to!

Contents

Preface

Hi! This is Kaavyaa, currently a grade 12 student at DPS Sector 45, Gurgaon and an alumnus of The Shri Ram School Aravali and Greenwood High. An eloquent writer and poet, fitness freak and trained kathak dancer, I also enjoy playing Basketball, and Badminton in my free time. You will often spot me waveboarding around the house or ranting about my hyperactive energy!

I actually hadn't discovered my passion for poetry writing until I had to write one for a project in sixth grade. But once I did, it was as if nothing could make me stop. This book comprises of a few of the poems I wrote from grades 6-10, mainlly based on my takes from the real world!

Acknowledgements

I want to express my gratitude to everyone who made this book happen. To notion press for successfully publishing this book, my sister, Reynah Gupta for her artwork, my friend, Kobid Mukhopadhyay for typing my poems and my parents, Kavita Jain and Deepak Gupta for their constant guidance and support.

This is my first book. I thank all those of you who are reading this right now to have bought this and shown interest in it. It would not have been possible without your love.

"A project is a work of a million"

There is an infinite number of people I am grateful to. Although I can't list them all here, does not mean they have any less value than the ones I could.

Keep making this happen readers. In anticipation of another book, thank you forever!

-Kaavyaa

1. Just Have Faith

We all pass through crests and troughs in our life, this poem is just a reminder to all to have faith even in the darkest times. No phase lasts for too long; and in the end, everything will be okay, and if it's not, it's not the end.

Sometimes in life, you will be hurt,
By people who want to see you so,
They will only take advantage,
And leave you shattered without hope.
But never, ever cry or sulk,
Over these fake friends,
Cause they will only feel a sense of victory,
And never want to make amends.
Just have faith, and stay put,
Cause what happened to you will happen to them,
This is just karma, the way of the world,
One from which no one's exempt.
And for all those who made others suffer,
It'll come down on you even rougher,
All the victims remain strong,
You will shine, and someday feel like
You do belong.

2. Republic Day

Just a salute to our freedom fighters and all the soldiers standing at the borders, far from their dear ones, letting us live fearlessly. Thank you!

On this auspicious day,

We are free to study and play.

Our constitution was formed,

For this day everyone had longed.

We salute our past freedom fighters,

To have seen this day without the Britishers.

The Britishers were quite proud,

But we successfully threw them out.
So here we stand with our rights,
On this auspicious day with pride.

• 3 •

3. Dear Teacher

This poem is a shoutout to all the teachers who have made us what we are today; taught us to think outside the box, imagine beyond the walls of the classroom and what not! They have been like our parents at school, and this poem is for all of them, expressing my gratitude, and listing the things I never got to say.

A teacher,

Is not just an educator,

But one who teaches us life values so fine,

Which to express, I can't find words to rhyme.

Through crests and troughs, we all pass,

And all this, they help us surpass,

With a smiling face all year round,

And a few scoldings also filling up the town.

Spoon-feeding they've got us used to,

I'm sure we'll miss it in a day or two,

On graduating from high school,

The only remaining safe tool.

Dear teacher,

To say this, I may not be a quotidian preacher,

But all your words so clever,

Are like beautiful footprints etched in my heart forever.

Great teachers like you,

Are the ones that inspire us too,

To do extraordinary things someday,

And some gratitude back, we will repay.

What a good teacher writes,

On the blackboard of life,

Can never be erased and stays in tight.

Dear teacher,

Thank you for your precious time,

Teaching us life values so fine,

To explain, I don't have words to rhyme.

4. Grade 7

Every year of our life, we learn something new, something different, which nurtures us to be the person we are today. Unlike stated in the poem, I faced innumerable ups and downs, but in the end I was glad to see myself evolve stronger than ever after facing them!

This has been an amazing year,

with so many wonderful cheers.

It has been a lovely time,

And we have gone one step higher,

on the knowledge ladder we have to climb.

This year has been a lot of fun,

with cheerful songs that we have sung.

This has been an amazing year,

with so many wonderful cheers!

5. In the examination hall

After submitting the papers, we had an hour in class with nothing except our pencil box. We were merely supposed to wait for the people who got extra time due to some specific reason to finish their papers too! So rather than wasting this precious hour, I observed and penned everything I saw happening around me!

I am writing this in the examination hall,
What do others do after finishing their papers and have nothing to stall?
I observe and write,
Some play sharpener fights.
Some stare at the floor,
And feel like walking out of the wooden door.
Most put their hoods down and go to sleep,

Without snoring, as quietly as sheep.
One draws circles so fine,
Others have unpredictable thoughts going on in their minds.
Few play with pens with eyes open wide,
While others just sit and revise.
Two naughty ones pass chits of paper,
Whereas others just giggle looking at the teacher.
These were the few things I noticed in the examination hall,
What to do when you have nothing to do at all?

6. Real Freedom

15ᵗʰ August 1947. Does this date strike out? You might know it as Independence day when India gained freedom from the British. But is this the definition of freedom for us now? I don't think so......

As a student, in my opinion, freedom or joy is not what we get from Independence Day,
It is a feeling that we get after stressful exam days.
That is when we enjoy life,
Because to live it we have got every right.
We are free to cheer and play,

With nothing to come in our way.
After exams is when we really feel,
The tension and pressure lifted from head to heel.

7. Happiness to me is

In our hectic lives, it becomes vital to find out where our happiness lies; which in turn helps us mitigate the sorrows and dark times. Be it spending time with friends and family, hard work, sports or just the memories, it is essential to find what makes us happy and thus embrace it...

Happiness,

It's a peculiar word you know,

What do you think about it though,

When it just pops up and leaves you so?

Is it being with friends and family,

With the loved ones on your side?

Or meeting a long lost friend,

Who then helps you see the light.

Or is it success that leaves you so,

Proud of yourself, regardless of how young or old.

But again, what exactly is success?

For another poem, I'll leave that to be told.

I think it's about the tiny little things,

Taking place in our day to day lives.

From a first basket to a friendly bet,

Which we don't always notice when the moment is ripe.

Or is it just the memories,

That leaves a smile on your face.

When you think about the past,

With nostalgia in every race.

Be it friends, memories or success,

But in our hectic lives, it becomes crucial too,

To find out where our happiness lies,

Which then goes on to lift our mood.

8. Hansel and Gretel: The Real One

If you are reading this right now, you have probably finished half the book, or well you have just jumped straight onto this one as it caught your eye; but either way, this is more of a light-weighted poem based on a twist to a childhood bedtime story just to lift your mood if you were too filled with emotions from the previous ones!

People think they know this story,
I'll tell you the real one, don't you worry.
The story all read, the one all know,
Was cooked up years and years ago.
Mind you the first bit gets to stay,
The bit where in the middle of the day,
Hansel and Gretel were left alone,

And couldn't find their way back home.
In the jungle, they roamed alone,
And reached a place far from home.
They saw a lady as thin as a stick,
Hung by two men whose pets were chicks.
They looked as scary as tigers,
And the chicks seemed afraid of these fighters.
Hansel and Gretel thought of rescuing her from the wicked,
Because to trap her, they surely had no ticket.
They were hiding behind the lush green bushes,
And picked stones from the ground, unseen by the wicked,
They threw stones when the men were off guard,
The men were frightened, and away did they dart!
Wounded were they and started to bleed,
Hurray! The lady was finally freed.
Petrified, the men ran away,
But forgot about the gold box kept on a tray.
The amount of gold was good for a lifetime,
The value of the box, almost divine.
The lady was Mathilda, mother their own,
Encaged by none other than their step-mom.
Merry together, they ran to their hut,
The witch in their home had to be chucked.
The moment they all reached their hut,
Stepmother Ellen was a roasted mut.
Mathilda exclaimed that Ellen was a witch,
The family, she had tried to trick.
Ellen then vanished into thin air,
No longer did the family have to care.

The gold box gave them a good life,
No longer did they have to strive!

9. Winter

Pleasant weather all year round, with the coldest weather in Bangalore merely requiring a thin hoodie, winters almost didn't exist! This made me miss the winter traditions in Gurgaon to such a great extent that it felt next to impossible to live the summer to the fullest either.

Winter has never exactly been what you call my "favourite season".
Summer has always existed and that's probably the reason.
But as I think of it now,
I kinda miss it somehow,
Cause without the cold,
How will you get the cosy cuddles that never grow old?
Think about the bonfire,

Around which we all sat in casual attire,

Roasting the soft marshmallows,

Reaping the taste as we sow.

It was the season when we enjoyed warm food,

With the hot cocoa which we brew,

And the smooth and delectable vegetable stew.

Clothes then might have been the tedious bit,

But friend, you have to admit,

It was kinda fun layering all your favourite clothes into one outfit.

Lastly, what is Christmas without the winter,

From fur coats to beanies, making us linger,

Around the Christmas tree with no whimper,

All this solely in winter.

Hence pals in conclusion,

Although summer is my favourite season,

But just like you can't enjoy the day without the night,

Summer's no fun without the winter's sight!

10. Change

Individuals usually fear changes and prefer staying in their comfort zone. But perhaps the best thing for one is out there into the unknown, and one just needs to search for it. This poem describes my initial consternation at moving from a place I had spent my entire life in(Gurgaon) to one I never knew existed till I studied Geography(Bangalore). In 2022, we shifted back to Gurgaon after spending just 2 years there. However, Bangalore was a fantasy, an area I never wanted to visit at first but happened to adore more than any other place in the world.

One knows change does take place,
In every human and animal race,
Like the change of us humans from an ape
And my shift is happening till late.
This shift has been a gigantic change,
From Gurgaon to Bangalore main.
The people differ,
The cats bicker,
The school's worse,
The house better.
Missing my old friends, I am quite sad,
Though it might not have been all that bad.
I have made new friends and fit in now,
So I guess it will be ok somehow.
To deal with things, I have learnt,
For that a badge, I have earned,
But change like this you know must be,
In every soul's life daily.

11. Sports

Sports have always been something I turn to when I'm stressed, or just need to clear my head cause when I'm playing, my mind is just focused on the game and the feeling is like no other. It is one that I want everyone to be able to cherish in their lives. This poem is thus a wake-up call for all those out there, glued to their screens and missing out on all this.

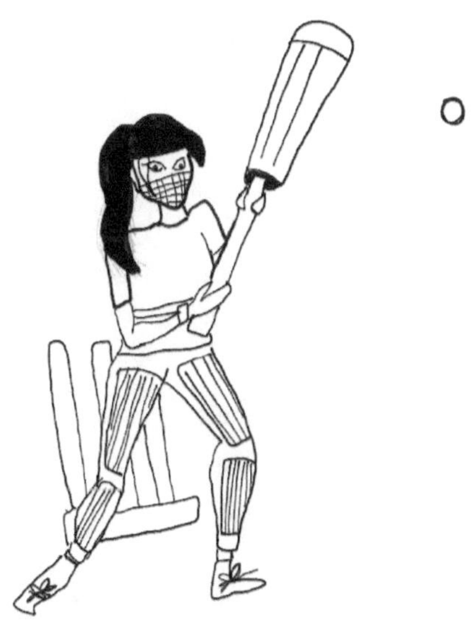

Innumerous sports exist in the world,

Ranging from hockey and cricket to volleyball.

Before they were played and loved by all,

Played with bats, sticks, rackets and balls.

What did people not play with?

How long will it stay till it's just a myth?
Now its significance is falling down,
Due to technology, the fans all drowned,
Despite this, I hope they remain,
For our children, the hobby main,
Let us not stick to screens all day,
Because all it does is make our eyes see vague,
Eyes are a gift from God, so this very May,
Don't wander about, but go to play.
I assure you it'll be a lot of fun,
With friends and family, just go and play in the sun!

12. Safari

This is just something I thought was essential to address. The beauty of wildlife and nature is breathtaking, it soothes and comforts us. However, all we humans are doing is killing them. So, the next time you eat non-vegetarian food or buy something just to flaunt, give this a thought...

In 2013, to Jim Corbett, I went,

Not only did I get to stay in a tent,

But also a safari van and driver we did rent.

Infinite deers, birds and all saw I,

But none really caught my eye,

As much as a wildcat's paw prints on the floor,

On the return journey along the road.

Forthwith the driver halted the van then,

Advised us to remain quiet unlike chickens in a pen.

Just then, a tiger paced,

My heart raced,

It schlepped a prey in its mouth,

The victim could no longer scream or shout.

Completely astonished the sight left me,

Thus, it could invariably be,

That I would desire to go on a safari another time,

And in just five years, the chance was mine!

Again went I,

With a joyous face,

But fie,

None had cared to save their grace.

Barely any fauna saw I,

Pity, nothing to catch my eye.

With rapid industrialization and urbanization,

We, humans, have forgotten the sensation,

That one gets on seeing wildlife in their natural estate,

But now, and now, all that is put at stake.

Fauna has become the bait,

For our wicked human race.

For all future generations,

I'm sorry due to urbanization.

This wealth you will not feel,

By just staring at a movie screen.

To preserve the world now is the time,

When we must step up and fight,

For the Earth which we care about the most,

And escalate wildlife's survival hopes.

Now is the time, we must fight,

And aid in the recovery of fauna's pitiable plight.
So let us rejuvinate the world, and not erase,
Our wildlife's race, no matter what it takes,
And make this world a better place!

13. 8-B

We often don't realise how much we love something until it's over. We usually don't comprehend its value until it's time to move on. Likewise, I was oblivious of how much I liked 8th until 9th came to an end. It is funny what you hold on to, and the things you recall when everything terminates.

Eighth grade was my favourite school year,
Having to leave that class certainly shed tears.
About 8B, infinite memories I behold,
I revere them as they unfold.

At the start, we were a monotonous class,
Missing seventh as the first month passed.
Then is when we started opening up,
To become a section eternally loved.
During free time in the back corner, we would sit,
Telling horror stories that were probably just myths.
Various stories I still remember,
Ranging from the 'red crayon' to 'missing murders'.
With Shivani ma'am and in-class DJ,
Other sections were sure to feel J.
Every short break, riff off we would play,
Until Advait would come and ruin the day.
Oh my god, how much I loved,
When to our faces, Anant's bakes were shoved.
All the teachers lay dumbstruck,
When Parth's intelligence did erupt.
One entertaining sight was dread,
When one witnessed Advait and Ainesh's catfight,
Once one dumped the bin onto the other's head,
Leaving him in a piteous plight.
Armaan was our class's jester,
The main in-class comedy maker.
8B backstage was performing arts,
With judges, hosts and Anant's tarts,
Various performances we would enact,
United as a blissful pact.
To date I really miss,
Expectation vs reality's bliss,
It was a Sanika and Ananya starrer,

Hilarious memories it did empower.

Our class though had one tradition,

Sometimes in plain recognition,

When we didn't feel like studying,

Informal school song and happy birthday we'd start singing.

Informal school song-

Everywhere where we go, x2

People want to know, x2

Who we are, x2

Where we come from, x2

So we tell them, x2

We are the Ramites, x2

Mighty mighty Ramites, x2

One and only ramites x2

[hooting – whoo!!!]

8B I still hold onto,

And each and every minute or two,

When I read this poem again,

I hop back on that plane,

To the place which used to be,

The one and only, 8B!

14. That Ding-Dong Moment

This is yet another poem I wrote in the examination hall based on probably the best phase of our existence, i.e., school life. To everyone who was ever a student, reading this will surely revive flashbacks of some old, sweet memories!

The moment the bell goes ding-dong-ding,
The students are out with a bing.
The soothing silence is now transformed,
With the loud chattering noises of students all around.
Everyone's walking out with their bags,
On hearing the sound, without any lag.
Some laughter heard about,
Cheers and sorrows also fill the town!
The whistle of the guards below,
Indicating the students from head to toe.
To go home and not stay there all day,
Because later for getting late, in front of parents they'll have no say,
Once all are gone, it doesn't seem,
Like anyone was ever-present at the scene.
I am sure this is what happens in every school ring,
The moment the bell goes ding-dong-ding!

15. Second Best Sister in the World

I feel all siblings will relate when I say that even though we tease each other, hit each other, and perhaps even blame each other even when it's our fault; at the end of the day, we love each other more than anything in the world, although we might not accept it when questioned. To be honest, contrary to the poem, I feel she is a way better sister than me but here goes.....

Reynah, we fight, scream and argue,

But are back as best friends in a minute or two.

With you I always am myself,

Be it singing dumb songs or partying with elves.

You know exactly how to make me laugh,

Even when I feel like chaff.

Being without you, all alone,

Is like being without my heart and soul.

No matter what, I want you to know,

That I love you for who you are from head to toe.

You are intelligent, cute funny and wise,

And on the moments we share, no one can put a price.

You and I will never be apart,

Maybe in distance but not in my heart.

About each other, we both complain,

And it still is fun to put you to blame!

The struggles and hardships that come our way,

We will face united as we have up till date.

Though sadly for you, no matter how hard you try,

I am a friend you can never get rid of even when we die.

You are the luckiest, but still the second-best sister in the world, why did you know?

It is because you have the best sister in the world you dumbo!

Afterword

No one said life is easy. But nobody ever said it was going to be hard either.

We are all living and just mere spectators to the days passing by, but are we just bystanders? Are we simply alive or are we actually living life to the fullest? Some days are eventful; whereas, others are just indifferent. When there is so much on everyone's plate besides countless sensations, be it happiness, sorrow, guilt, or any one of the other twenty-seven emotions, where do we let it all out? Where do we vent?

That is where poetry comes into frame, and is exactly what got me to write this book. Sentiments can be scary. One could be on cloud nine right now but feel completely forlorn the very next second.

You may have cried with me in one of the touching poems or simply related to an event bringing a smile to your face. In whatever ways, I wish this helped you feel something, allowed your heart to pour out and assured you that there are peaks and valleys in everyone's lives, and significantly, we need to be ready to help us help ourselves. You are enough. More than enough. Ready to take on the world, and rock the show.

I end this here; elated for you made it so far into the book, be on the lookout for the next one.

In anticipation of publishing my next work, keep making this happen readers!

Thanking you, always and forever,

Kaavyaa.